Quick & easy

Dwarf

Hamster

Care

T.F.H. Publications
One TFH Plaza
Third and Union Avenues
Neptune City, NJ 07753

This book has been published with the intent to provide accurate and authoritative
information in regard to the subject matter within. While every precaution has been
taken in preparation of this book, the publisher and author assume no responsibility
for errors or omissions. Neither is any liability assumed for damages resulting from
the use of the information herein.

ISBN 0-7938-1027-2

www.tfh.com

Table
of Contents

You and Your Dwarf Hamster

C ongratulations on bringing home your dwarf hamster! You have just acquired a delightful and friendly pet that will bring you much joy and entertainment for the next few years.

Dwarf hamsters are adorable little animals that have been kept as pets in the US for more than 30 years. Dwarf hamsters are not just miniatures of the commonly kept Golden or Syrian hamster; they are distinct species with different looks, habits, and pet qualities.

Dwarf Hamsters as Pets
Dwarf hamsters are active and entertaining pets. They sometimes

Dwarf hamsters are not just miniature versions of the commonly kept Syrian hamster but are a distinct species of their own. Their small size captivates people of all ages.

walk upright on their hind feet and perform flips. When you place your hand into a cage of dwarf hamsters, they will often run up to your hand to investigate.

Their small size appeals to both adults and children who are captivated by the hamster's cute roly-poly looks. Dwarf hamsters are inexpensive, undemanding, and easy to care for. They can be kept in their cage full-time as long as they are provided a spacious, entertaining (toy-filled) cage in which to play. They can be as relaxing to watch as an aquarium of tropical fish. Hamsters can even remain unattended in their cage with extra food and water over the weekend.

Handling

Dwarf hamsters are not "cuddly" pets. Tame dwarf hamsters do not mind being petted, but they also do not like being held for long periods of time. Dwarf hamsters typically bite only when they are afraid or threatened. Gentle regular handling will make dwarf hamsters docile and reduce the likelihood of them biting a human. With frequent handling and attention, most hamsters become tame and make good pets. However, it requires time, patience, and a food treat to win their trust.

Nocturnal Noises

At night, dwarf hamsters may make a lot of noise, including gnawing, cracking seeds, drinking water, and running on their exercise wheels. When your dwarf hamsters play-fight with each other you are likely to hear their soft squeals and chatter.

dwarf hamster is very clean and performs an elaborate grooming ritual several times a day. The hamster first licks his front feet, or hands. Then, using both hands, he washes his face and behind his ears. Using a hind foot, the hamster delicately cleans the inside of his ears and then nibbles clean his toes. The hamster continues washing the fur all over his body and then licks his hind toes after scratching with them. A dwarf hamster is very fastidious, and may set up a separate toilet area in his cage.

How Many?

A dwarf hamster can be kept by itself, or you can keep them in small groups. Do not mix the different species of dwarf hamsters together, as they will aggressively fight and may even kill each other. Dwarf

Dwarf hamsters who are housed together with others of the same species are usually more active and playful than those that are kept alone.

hamsters tend to be more active and playful when housed with others of their own kind. A hamster kept alone tends to be less active, sleeps more, and, therefore, is less interesting. If you want to keep more than one dwarf hamster, you must buy young hamsters (less than eight weeks old) at the same time, so that they can grow up together. The hamsters do not need to be littermates but should be approximately the same size to avoid bullying by a larger animal. The hamsters can be kept in single sex or mixed-sex groups. Naturally, if you have more than one hamster, you must also buy a large enough cage and provide numerous nest boxes and other hiding places.

The Different Species
There are four species of dwarf hamsters kept as pets in the US. Some differences between the species are discussed below.

Chinese Striped Hamster
- *Other common names:* striped hamster, ratlike hamster
- Description: 4 to 5 inches in length, grayish-brown with a black dorsal stripe, juveniles are sometimes grayer than adults, and their fur feels silky

The Winter-white hamster is easy to tame and seems to enjoy being petted. This species is very friendly, active, and energetic.

Quick & Easy Dwarf Hamster Care

- *Country of Origin:* China

Young, untamed Chinese hamsters can be nervous, and adults that are not used to people can be difficult to tame. However, once tame, individuals tend to become calm and are easily handled. Like a mouse, the Chinese hamster uses its short prehensile tail and paws to cling to its owner's fingers. Compared to the other dwarf hamsters, the Chinese is a relatively good climber and jumper. This species can be aggressive with other hamsters.

Winter-white and Campbell's Hamster

At one time the Campbell's Russian hamster and the Winter-white hamster were considered the same species, but later researchers showed they were distinct species. Some hobbyists have bred the two species together, and the resulting hybrid offspring are often infertile.

Campbell's Russian hamster
- *Other common names:* Djungarian hamster, striped hamster, hairy-footed hamster
- *Description:* 3 to 4 inches in length, gray brown color, white belly, thick woolly feeling coat
- *Country of Origin:* Northern China, Mongolia, central Asia, southern Siberia

Winter-white Hamster
- *Other common names:* Siberian hamster, striped hairy-footed hamster, and Winter-white Russian hamster
- *Description:* about 4 inches in length, gray color with a white belly. As the days become shorter in fall and winter (less than eight hours of light each day), the gray coat molts into solid white. The white color helps to camouflage them against the snow and protect them from potential predators.
- *Country of Origin:* Mongolia, Manchuria, Siberia, and sections of China

You and Your Dwarf Hamster

These two species are grouped together because they tend to behave similarly as pets. With consistent interactions, these species are relatively easy to tame. Once tame, they are friendly, confident, and curious. Many individuals seem to enjoy being petted. These species are also active and like to run and move about.

Roborovskii's Hamster

- *Other common names:* desert hamster
- *Description:* 2 inches in length, sandy brown with a white belly, white marks above their eyes look like eyebrows, white whiskers on their snout make them look like unshaven.
- *Country of Origin:* Mongolia, China, and Russia

This smallest species of pet hamster is also the fastest. The Roborovskii's hamster must be held in cupped hands and continually walked between the hands. Because they are so small and so fast, they are difficult for many pet owners to handle. If they escape while being held, they can be especially difficult to catch. This species can sometimes jump one foot straight up in the air.

Dwarf Hamsters in the Wild

There are 24 species of hamsters, and hamsters are found in Europe, the Middle East, Russia, and China. Most species live in arid, desert-like habitats. Hamsters are small, between two to four inches in length, with tiny tails that are barely visible. However, hamsters in the genus *Cricetulus*, (including the Chinese hamster), have longer tails. Hamsters live in long underground burrows that they dig with their sharp claws. They dig separate chambers for sleeping, storing food, and a bathroom. Hamsters have long whiskers that help them navigate underground as well as aboveground.

Dwarf hamsters have expandable cheek pouches in which to carry food and bedding to their burrows for storage.

Untamed individuals of this species do not tend to bite as readily as do the other dwarf species. Once tame, they become somewhat calmer, but Roborovskii's hamster is a very active animal. Since most children like to hold their pets, this is the least suitable dwarf species to consider for children. This species is the least common dwarf hamster pet.

Cheek Pouches

The word "hamster" comes from the German verb, "hamstern," which means to hoard. Hamsters have expandable cheek pouches that they use to carry food and bedding back to their burrows. Food is usually collected in one pouch at a time. When enough desirable food is available, a hamster may fill his pouches to the bursting point. The full pouches will extend past the hamster's shoulders and make him look misshapen. Hamsters use their front paws to fill their pouches and use them to squeeze the food out of their cheek pouches. Hamsters are able to carry and store great quantities of food in their underground storage chambers. This adaptation allows the hamster to survive on stored food when food is scarce. Hamsters spend the winter in hibernation in their burrows, only waking on warmer days to eat food from their pantry.

Teeth

When a piece of food is too large, a hamster will use his large incisors to carry the item. A dwarf hamster has two pairs of chisel-like incisors in the front of its mouth. These teeth never stop growing. The incisor teeth enable a hamster to easily open hard seeds, grains, and nuts. A hamster's teeth are constantly worn down when it gnaws and chews on hard substances. If you look at a hamster's front teeth, you will notice that the lower incisors are longer than the upper incisors. A hamster's molars do not keep growing.

Hamsters have powerful jaw muscles and teeth. They can easily gnaw through a variety of substances, including plastic and wood. Between a hamster's incisors and rear molars is a space called the diastema. When a hamster eats, its cheeks block this space to prevent any sharp food from being swallowed. Food enters the hamster's large cheek pouches from a hole in the diastema.

Dwarf hamsters have a keen sense of smell and communicate with each other through pheromones secreted from the scent-producing gland in the middle of their bellies.

Dwarf Hamster History

In 1930, a naturalist in Syria dug up a burrow containing a mother hamster and her litter for a researcher at Hebrew University in Jerusalem. The Syrian hamster then rose to worldwide prominence because it readily bred in captivity. Hamsters are extremely prolific. Within a year, there were more than 300 Syrian hamsters in the first laboratory colony. Within 20 years, the dwarf hamsters were also successfully reared in captivity. Dwarf hamsters are now found as pets all over the world.

Dwarf Hamster Senses

Dwarf hamsters have poor eyesight but have an acute sense of hearing. Aside from the squeaks that people can hear, hamsters can also communicate and hear sounds in the ultrasonic range, which people cannot hear. Scientists think ultrasonic sounds are important during mating.

A keen sense of smell helps dwarf hamsters locate food and detect pheromones, which dwarf hamsters use to communicate with each other in social interactions. Pheromones are chemicals secreted from the body that facilitate communication and influence behavior between members of the same species. Both male and female dwarf hamsters have a scent-producing gland in the middle of their belly, though the gland is larger in males than in females. It is not conspicuous, and the gland looks like a small hairless patch. The gland's scent is obvious to other dwarf hamsters, but you are unlikely to notice the smell. Besides using their belly gland, dwarf hamsters also mark their territory with urine and droppings. Dwarf hamsters can recognize individual hamsters and whether a hamster is a male or a female by smell.

Dwarf Hamster Varieties

All small animals kept in captivity eventually develop mutations

The Law

In some states, certain species of pets are not legal for pet stores to sell or for you to own. Although there is national legislation that governs the keeping of animals, individual states still have their own laws, and these laws vary from state to state and even from city to city. States can ban personal ownership of an animal species for various reasons. For example, in California, it is not legal to keep Chinese hamsters (*Cricetulus griseus*) as pets. The California Department of Fish and Game has banned this species because of concerns that if Chinese hamsters become established in the wild, they could damage crops and displace native wildlife. In general, if a hamster species is offered for sale in the pet stores within your state, it is probably legal for you to own the hamster, but check to make sure.

from their normal color. In the wild, animals that are unusual in color are more noticeable to predators and often do not live long enough to reproduce. Therefore, unusual colors are not typically found in wild populations. However, a conspicuous color is not a problem for pet animals, because people protect their pets from potential predators.

Similar to breeds of cats, the different varieties of dwarf hamsters differ from each other in color, markings, coat textures, and sometimes temperament. Pet stores usually do not stock a wide variety of dwarf hamsters. If you want a particular color or a particular species of dwarf hamster that proves hard to find, ask whether a pet store can special order the dwarf hamster for you from their suppliers. You can also contact the breeders listed on Internet sites devoted to dwarf hamsters and hamster clubs.

The Campbell's Russian hamster is available in more than two dozen different colors, including mottled black, lilac fawn, albino, champagne, black, argente, and blue, as well as their normal gray color. The eye color can be either black or red. This species can have the typical shorthaired coat, or they can have a satin coat, which is a very attractive as the fur has a high glossy sheen. Expect new colors and coat types to be developed.

The Winter-white hamster is available in only three colors. Besides the normal gray color, look for pearl and sapphire. The pearl hamster is white with black eyes, and is essentially the hamster's winter coat color. The sapphire is blue gray. Eye color is black and no coat differences have yet been developed.

Roborovskii's hamster is currently available only in its natural sandy brown color. The Chinese hamster is currently available in only two varieties: the normal-colored, and the dominant spot, which is white with patches of color.

The Campbell's Russian hamster is available in more than two dozen different colors and can have either the typical shorthaired coat or a glossy, satin coat.

Dwarf Hamsters and Children

Very young children always need to be watched when they are playing with a hamster. Dwarf hamsters are very small, and rough handling can frighten the hamster and cause him to bite. The child might then drop or throw the hamster, which can be fatal to the hamster. A parent can help reduce the risk of a bite by showing children how to properly hold their hamster and instructing them on what to do should their pet begin to wiggle, (for example, return the hamster to his cage). A parent might need to help take the hamster out of his cage for the child to visit with. Children should be told to open the cage and let the hamster come to them rather than trying to pull the hamster out of his home.

Nervous at First

When you first bring your dwarf hamsters home, they might be frightened and hide in their nest box. Some hamsters are more confident, and will readily investigate their new home. Either way, let your new pets settle down and get used to their new home. The first three weeks are the most stressful for hamsters as they adjust to a new environment. Talk to your hamsters but do not try to hold them. You can eventually offer your pets some of their food in your hand, but if they seem shy and nervous, leave them alone for a while or talk soothingly to them. Sometimes partially covering all but the front of their cage with a brown paper bag will help your hamsters feel more secure and less vulnerable as they will be able to detect less motion around their cage. Once they have become less nervous, you can completely remove the covering.

Housing Your Dwarf Hamster

Dwarf hamsters are very adept at escaping their enclosures and often become lost because someone forgets to securely close the cage door or because the hamsters chew out of their enclosure. Therefore, the cage you choose must be well constructed and escape-proof.

You can find a suitable cage for your dwarf hamster at a pet store. Dwarf hamsters can be housed in glass aquariums or wire-framed cages. The cage should measure at least 24 inches long by 12 inches wide by 10 inches high. Dwarf hamsters are not good climbers. They are ground dwellers and do best in a cage that provides plenty of floor space rather than in a tall cage with room to climb.

A Carrying Cage

The rectangular plastic enclosures with snap-on lids, sometimes called small animal habitats, are not typically large enough to house a pair of dwarf hamsters. They make suitable carrying cages to take your new pets home or to the veterinarian, and they provide a secure place to keep your pets while you are cleaning their cage, but they should not be a permanent home for dwarf hamsters. Be careful with these cages because, if you drop them, they will break.

The cage is the most expensive piece of equipment you will need to buy for your dwarf hamster. The general rule when buying a cage is to choose the largest cage you can afford. No matter what species, dwarf hamsters are very active animals and need a roomy home. A cage that is too small and confining will become dirty and smelly more quickly, and it can lead to fights among your pets who will become irritable without enough space. The more room you provide your pets in which to play and explore, the more interesting

When picking out a cage for your dwarf hamster, choose the largest one you can afford so you can provide your pet with plenty of space.

and healthy they will be. The cage you choose should be large enough to allow your dwarf hamsters room for separate eating, sleeping, and toilet areas, as well as one or two exercise wheels. A 10-gallon glass aquarium with a secure wire-screen cover will provide a good home for a pair of dwarf hamsters.

What Type of Cage?

Purchase a cage where the entire top lifts off, so that you can readily reach your pets. Compared to a wire-frame cage, an aquarium will keep the area around your pets' home tidy because shavings and other debris cannot spill out of the cage. However, the glass sides can become dirty and difficult to see through if they are not kept clean.

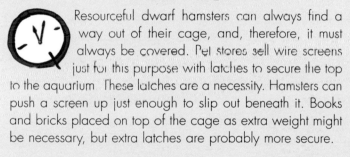

Prevent Escapes

Resourceful dwarf hamsters can always find a way out of their cage, and, therefore, it must always be covered. Pet stores sell wire screens just for this purpose with latches to secure the top to the aquarium. These latches are a necessity. Hamsters can push a screen up just enough to slip out beneath it. Books and bricks placed on top of the cage as extra weight might be necessary, but extra latches are probably more secure.

If you choose a glass aquarium or plastic small animal habitat, keep in mind that these types of housing are not as well ventilated as a wire cage. While these cages are beneficial because they are not drafty, poor ventilation and lax cleaning habits can cause ammonia gas to build up to uncomfortable levels. This can irritate your hamster's respiratory system. For your pets' health, you must be vigilant in keeping such a cage clean. If you can smell your pets' home, then it is certainly an unhealthy environment for them, especially because they are right on top of the smelly bedding. If you think you might be neglectful in cage cleaning chores, select a wire-frame cage instead. Also, keep in mind that aquariums are heavier

Cage Floors

Dwarf hamsters have tiny feet that can accidentally become caught and twisted in the wire floor of a metal cage. If the cage you choose has a wire floor rather than a solid floor, you must be certain to completely cover the floor with bedding to prevent this potential problem. Continuously walking on exposed, wire-cage bottoms can also cause your dwarf hamster's feet to become sore and irritated.

than wire cages and can be more difficult to move and clean.

The cage should have a large door opening that allows you to easily reach inside the cage and take your hamster out. Check that the door latches securely and cannot be easily pushed out at a corner by your pet's super-hamster strength. The best cages will have both a door and a removable top or side to provide easy access to the interior of the cage. A cage handle can make moving the cage easier.

A wooden cage is not recommended because they are difficult to keep clean and the wood absorbs urine and other odors.

Metal Cages

Wire cages do present a problem for owners of dwarf hamsters. Due to their small sizes, dwarf hamsters, especially young ones, can readily squeeze between the vertical bars of many rodent cages, even cages with bars that are only a half-inch apart. If your hamster can squeeze his head between the cage bars, the rest of his body will follow. For this reason, only choose a wire cage constructed with hatched wire mesh. Such cages are typically sold for mice. A potential drawback to a mouse cage is that mice do not need as much room as dwarf hamsters, and it can be difficult to find a mouse cage large enough for dwarf hamsters.

If you buy a wire cage with vertical bars that measure more than one-quarter inch apart, then you should also attach a heavy gauge wire mesh (not window screen!) that measures no greater than one-quarter inch square to the outside of the cage using metal clips. Do not use plastic ties, lightweight wire, or string to attach the additional wire mesh. These materials are not durable enough to withstand a dwarf hamster's chewing. The wire mesh should attach tightly to the original bars to prevent a hamster from squeezing between the two layers of wire and accidentally getting stuck.

Metal cages do have some other drawbacks. While wire cages provide good ventilation, they are also potentially drafty. Over time, a hamster's relatively concentrated urine can corrode the metal pan that fits beneath a wire cage. You can help prevent this problem by cleaning your pets' bathroom area every few days or by lining the tray bottom with foil (as long as your hamsters do not have access to the tray).

If you choose a wire-frame cage, try to find one with high bottom tray sides to catch bedding and other debris that your hamsters will kick out during their normal activities. You can also place the cage on top of newspaper that extends for several inches more than the cage's diameter, or place the cage inside a kitty litter pan to catch the

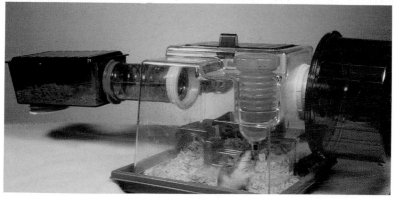

Colorful plastic housing with connecting tubes is an exciting way to make your pet's cage into a playground, but make sure the cage has plenty of ventilation.

material that spills out, or purchase a cloth seed guard sold in the bird section of a pet store.

Dwarf Hamster Playgrounds

Colorful plastic housing with connecting tubes allows you to expand your hamsters' cage into a playground. However, like aquariums, this type of housing provides less ventilation than wire cages. Tube housing can also become smelly if it is not cleaned frequently. Some dwarf hamsters can readily gnaw through the plastic tubes and escape. The plastic can also become dirty and difficult to see through, so it must be washed regularly.

If you want to use tube housing for your dwarf hamsters, be sure to choose a large enough cage and select a model with maximum ventilation and a door that is large enough for you to reach in and easily take out your pets. Some dwarf hamsters have a difficult time crawling up vertical tubes. Placing the tubes horizontally between the cage units can make it easier for your pets to move about.

Bedding is a necessary element of your dwarf hamster's housing. Bedding provides a warm, dry place for him to sleep and enables him to burrow.

Bedding

Your dwarf hamsters need bedding in their cage. Bedding is used to absorb moisture (from urine, and water from the occasional leaking bottle), reduce odors, and provide a warm dry place for your pets to sleep. A thick layer of bedding will allow your dwarf hamsters to engage in some of their natural behaviors, such as burrowing and building a sleeping nest. Pet stores carry a variety of small animal beddings

Ammonia

The ammonia vapors from urine that develop in your pets' cage can make owning hamsters less pleasant. The harsh smell is also uncomfortable for the hamsters. Ammonia is a severe irritant and is detrimental to the health of hamsters. It affects the mucous membranes of their eyes and respiratory tract. The health of hamsters with chronic respiratory conditions can worsen if they are regularly exposed to ammonia vapors, and it can make dwarf hamsters more susceptible to opportunistic infections. Hamsters housed on dirty, moist bedding are most susceptible to these effects, as are hamsters housed in aquariums that are infrequently cleaned. Help keep your dwarf hamster healthy and clean his cage often.

that are suitable for hamsters, including wood shavings, such as pine and aspen, and more sophisticated beddings made from recycled paper or wood pulp that are designed to help control or eliminate odor. The latter types are more expensive, but they can make it more pleasurable to own hamsters because their home is less likely to smell unpleasant between cage cleanings. Bedding made from recycled paper contains no harmful inks, dyes, or significant levels of heavy metals. Whatever bedding you choose, you only need a few inches of material to cover the floor. Make sure that the bedding completely covers the floor of a wire cage.

Ideally, small animal bedding should be dust-free. Dusty bedding can irritate a hamster's respiratory system or aggravate an existing respiratory ailment. Because hamsters live directly on their bedding, they are more likely to stir up fine particles and be at risk for these potential problems. In general, paper pulp and recycled paper products tend to be lower in dust compared to wood shavings.

The Cedar Shavings Controversy

Shavings made from softwoods, which include pine and cedar, are still the most common type of bedding for small pets such as hamsters. These beddings have been popular because they are relatively inexpensive and are often fragrant smelling, particularly cedar shavings. However, cedar shavings have been implicated as both causing and aggravating respiratory problems in small animals. In addition, they are known to affect liver function in rats and hamsters. Although not all experts agree that cedar shavings present a risk to small pets, a growing body of evidence seems to support hobbyists' contentions that cedar shavings can be unhealthy for small animals. Therefore, cedar shavings are not recommended for your dwarf hamsters.

Cage Accessories

Your dwarf hamster will need several cage accessories, such as food dishes, a hanging water bottle, a nest box, and toys. You can find a wide array of dwarf hamster accessories at your local pet shop.

Purchase a food dish that is heavy, such as a ceramic dish, so that your dwarf hamster cannot tip it over and spill the contents.

Food Dishes

If you have a metal cage, you can attach the dishes to the side to prevent your dwarf hamsters from tipping them over and spilling the contents. If you use a freestanding dish, make sure it is heavy enough that your hamsters cannot tip it over. Pet stores sell a variety of colorful ceramic dishes that are too heavy for hamsters to move. Placing their food in a dish instead of on the cage floor will prevent your pets' food from becoming accidentally contaminated with droppings and urine.

The Water Bottle

Provide your hamsters with fresh water, using a gravity-fed water bottle sold at pet stores. A special holder, also available at pet stores, enables you to hang the water bottle in an aquarium. Do not use an open dish to provide your dwarf hamsters with water. The hamsters will fill an open container of water with their cage bedding, and the water will become unsanitary and unsuitable for drinking. The increased moisture from a spilled dish of water can create an unhealthy, damp environment, especially in an aquarium-type cage. In case the water bottle leaks, do not place it over your pet's food dish. The bottle's water tube should be a comfortable height for your hamsters to easily reach up and drink from, but should not be so low to the cage floor that bedding could contact the tube and cause the bottle to leak.

A Nest Box

Each dwarf hamster needs a nesting box for sleeping and security. This "bedroom" gives your pets a safe hiding place where they can retreat away from loud noises and any disturbing activity outside their cage. You can buy a nesting box at a pet store. A variety of types are sold, including ones that are made to satisfy a small animal's natural instinct to chew, such as fruit-flavored cardboard tunnels, huts made from natural plant fibers, and wooden blocks that a pet hollows out. Other kinds are less destructible and are made of ceramic or hard plastic. You can also make your pets a nest

Nesting Material

Give your dwarf hamsters unscented tissue paper or paper towels to shred into nesting material. Shredding paper into a nest is a favorite activity among hamsters. Pet stores also sell nesting material that you can use. However, do not buy artificial fiber bedding sold for birds and hamsters. The small fibers can wrap around a hamster's feet and cut off circulation, thus causing the loss of a limb.

box from an old cereal box or cardboard milk carton. Once the box becomes chewed up or smelly, you will need to replace it.

Where to Keep the Cage

Your dwarf hamsters should be part of your family. Place their cage in a location where you can watch and enjoy them. The cage should be kept in an active, yet not too busy area of your home. Make the cage a pleasant part of the room. Place the cage on a dresser or table with some attractive fabric beneath it. The floor is not the most ideal location, as the temperature near the floor is often cooler than on a dresser or table. On top of a high shelf is also not ideal, because it will be too high for you to enjoy your pets.

Do not place your pets' cage near a heating or air conditioning vent, a drafty window, or in direct sunlight. Dwarf hamsters are susceptible to overheating, chills, and drafts. Hamsters can tolerate a house's normal variations in room light, temperature, and

Hamsters are enthusiastic gnawers. Do not leave any items such as clothing or papers on or near your pets' cage. Anything that can be pulled into the cage will be chewed on and destroyed.

Quick & Easy Dwarf Hamster Care

humidity. Room temperatures between 65 and 72 degrees Fahrenheit with humidity between 40 and 50 percent provide satisfactory living conditions for your dwarf hamsters.

You should never keep your pets in a garage or an unfinished basement. Not only is it unhealthy for your dwarf hamsters due to automobile exhaust or other fumes, but the temperature is more extreme and variable (both too cold and too hot), and your pets are more likely to be neglected.

Hamsters do not like bright lights. Therefore, do not place your pets' cage next to a table, floor, or overhead light. Your dwarf hamster's cage should be placed out of the direct view of the family cat and dog. Your hamsters can become nervous and stressed if a dog or cat can constantly sniff and stare at them. In addition, dwarf hamsters might be sensitive to the ultrasonic sounds produced by computers and television sets. Therefore, do not place your pets' home near computers or televisions.

Cage Accessories

Your dwarf hamster will need the following cage accessories. Many different varieties are sold at your local pet shop.
- food dishes
- hanging water bottle
- nesting box
- nesting material
- toys

Toys

An exercise wheel is mandatory for dwarf hamsters. Your dwarf hamsters can run for hours and will log several miles on their wheels each night. Freestanding wheels made of either plastic or metal are sold for use in aquariums or wire cages. Dwarf hamsters can get their small feet caught in wire-frame exercise wheels, so you should only buy an exercise wheel with a solid floor. Such wheels are commonly sold in pet stores, or they can be special ordered.

Hamsters housed with toys are more active and interesting to watch, and the animals are content and happier. Pet stores sell a variety of toys that can be made into a playground for hamsters. Give your pets toys designed for hamsters and other small rodents, such as wood chew sticks, tunnels, and ladders. Many wooden toys made for parakeets and parrots are also safe to use with your dwarf hamsters. Wood chews keep hamsters busy and active and provide a hard surface for them to gnaw, which helps to keep their teeth in good shape. However, wooden objects will also absorb urine and other odors and will need to be replaced when they become smelly and old. If your pets are housed in an aquarium, you can increase the area available for your hamsters by adding ladders and platforms.

Alternating toys is a trick that dog and cat owners have used for years, and can be used by hamster owners as well. Let your hamsters play with a toy for a week, then take it away and replace it with a new toy. The following week you can temporarily take away the new toy and replace it with the old one. By switching your pets' toys

Make Your Own Toys

You can also find suitable toys for your pets in your home. Give your dwarf hamsters the cardboard rolls from empty toilet paper or paper towels. You can partially bury these tubes under your pets' bedding and create a system of tunnels for them to explore. Be creative and connect multiple roles and make multiple entrances and exits. Cardboard egg cartons also provide entertaining play for hamsters. Hamsters will chew on whatever you put in their cage, so be sure the items are safe.

An exercise wheel is a necessity for dwarf hamsters, keeping them in shape and healthy.

around, your hamsters will stay active and interested in exploring their environment.

Cleaning the Cage

A clean cage plays an important role in keeping your hamsters healthy. Plan on cleaning your pets' cage once or twice a week. The more hamsters kept in a cage, especially in a cage that is relatively small, the more often the cage will need to be cleaned. If your hamsters are housed in a very large cage, such as a 20-gallon aquarium, then it is reasonable to consider cleaning the cage less often than twice a week. A hamster's small, hard droppings do not smell bad, but their urine can develop a pungent smell from ammonia. Ammonia is a severe irritant and is detrimental to the health of hamsters. No pet should be housed on dirty, wet bedding. Your hamster's cage will only smell if you do not clean it often enough. Ideally, you should clean your pets' cage before it becomes smelly. If the area around your pets' cage smells offensive, it is past time to clean the cage.

How to Clean the Cage

To clean your hamster's cage, completely change the bedding in the cage and replace it with fresh, clean bedding. In between cleanings, you can do a partial cage change. Your dwarf hamsters will establish one or two toilet areas in their cage, which can make cage cleaning easier. Try placing your hamsters' food dish, water bottle, and nest box at one end of their cage. This will help your hamsters establish a bathroom area away from their sleeping and eating areas. If your pets do use a cage corner for a bathroom area, the bedding in this area can be replaced every few days or so. Doing so will help reduce odor and keep the cage cleaner and more sanitary. Each week,

Toys make dwarf hamsters content and happy, so provide your pets with toys designed for hamsters and other small rodents, such as ladders, tunnels, and chew sticks.

Keep your dwarf hamster's food dish, water bottle, and nest box separate from his bathroom area to help keep the cage clean and sanitary.

partially or completely (if it smells or is dirty) replace the nesting material in each hamster's nest box. Less often, you will need to wash or replace some of your pets' toys and their nest boxes when they become chewed and tattered.

Once a month, do a thorough cleaning. Wash the cage with hot, soapy water. Be sure to rinse and dry it thoroughly. If necessary, disinfect the cage with a bleach solution, consisting of one tablespoon of bleach for each gallon of cold water. Wash the water bottle, food dish, and any plastic toys. Wood toys can eventually splinter if washed in water, but scraping them clean with a file is also effective. Scrape or file off any grime that might have accumulated on the bars of a wire cage.

You will need to place your pets in a secure container, such as a plastic carrying cage (small animal habitat) while you clean their home. Some hamster owners place their pets in their nest box

The Familiar Scent of Home

Dwarf hamsters often become upset and frantically run around their home after it has been cleaned. While pet owners find the clean cage refreshing, hamsters are not often as enthusiastic. They like something with their scent on it and will often become quite busy marking their home again so that is smells better to them. Partial cage cleanings, such as replacing most, but not all of your hamsters' bedding and nesting material and not washing all of your pet's toys will satisfy your pets' need for something familiar.

within the bathtub during cage cleaning. The nest box provides a secure hiding place and the slippery sides of the bathtub are usually too steep for dwarf hamsters to jump or climb out.

Feeding Your Dwarf Hamster

Like people, dwarf hamsters are omnivorous, which means they eat both plant and animal foods. In the wild, dwarf hamsters will eat seasonally available seeds, including wheat, barley, millet, soybeans, and peas, as well as plant shoots, leaves, flowers, and root vegetables, including potatoes, carrots, and beets. Insects and other invertebrates such as spiders are also eaten and stored in a dwarf hamster's food chambers.

Feeding your dwarf hamsters a healthy balanced diet is considerably easy because a variety of commercial foods are sold for hamsters at pet stores. Nutrition is a key factor in promoting good health and a long life. A balanced diet for hamsters includes the appropriate amounts of proteins, carbohydrates, fats, vitamins, and minerals. All these nutrients interact in the building, maintenance, and functioning of a hamster's body. It is also important to feed a diet that does not contain too much or too little of these nutrients. The amount of protein your pets need is influenced by a number of physiological factors, including age. Hamsters need less protein when they are adults than they do when they are growing, pregnant, or nursing a litter of babies. A good diet for dwarf hamsters should contain between 16 and 20 percent protein.

Vitamins

Vitamins are necessary as catalysts for chemical reactions in the body. The vitamins that hamsters need to eat in their diet are different from those needed by people. For example, hamsters can make their own Vitamin C, while people must get it from an external source, such as oranges. A number of vitamins, including many B vitamins, are synthesized in hamsters by intestinal bacteria. These vitamins are available to hamsters by means of coprophagy, which is the eating of special droppings that contain the vitamins synthesized by the bacteria. Hamsters typically engage in this behavior at night or early in the morning, when you are not likely to observe them. Nonetheless, do not be concerned if you see your pets engaged in such behavior; coprophagy is necessary for their good health so do not prevent your dwarf hamsters from doing this.

Fats

Fats are a significant source of calories and energy. A good diet for hamsters should contain approximately five percent fat. Fats make up part of the structure of every cell and are necessary for absorption of fat-soluble vitamins, including Vitamins A, D, and E. Fats help to prevent and alleviate skin problems. A deficiency of fat can show up as scaly skin, or rough, thin hair.

Vitamin Supplements

Feeding your hamsters a fresh, high-quality diet will usually ensure adequate intake of necessary vitamins and minerals. Supplementation with a vitamin and mineral supplement, unless directed by your veterinarian, is unnecessary.

Fresh is Best

It is important that the food you feed your hamsters is fresh. Food that is old can become stale and lose some of its nutritional value. Packaged foods should be fresh and sweet smelling, not rancid or dusty. Do not buy a large amount of food, because it will take too long to use all of it. Some manufacturers stamp a date on food bags and recommend that the food be used within one year of this date. Store your hamsters' food in a cool, dry environment. Sunlight, heat, and time will degrade the vitamins in a food, so keep your pets' food in an airtight container, such as a glass jar with a lid, or be sure to completely close a package that is self-sealing.

Suggested Diets

Feed your pets one of the rodent mixes sold at pet stores for hamsters and gerbils. These mixes contain seeds, grains, beans, nuts, alfalfa pellets, dried fruits and vegetables, and sometimes various type of kibble. Do not choose a food that is mostly sunflower seeds or other nuts; such a diet will allow your hamsters to become malnourished and overweight. Dwarf hamsters enjoy picking through their food and eating their favorite items first. Since a food's nutritional analysis is based on consumption of the entire mix of ingredients, a selective eater may not be getting a nutritious, complete diet. Over time, this "selective feeding" can cause inadequate nutrition and obesity. While it is reasonable not to expect your dwarf hamsters to like some items in their food, consistently refusing to eat more than half of a food's ingredients is not healthy. You can thwart your dwarf hamsters' selective feeding

Food mixes formulated for gerbils and hamsters are perfect for your dwarf hamster, but do not choose a food that is mostly nuts or sunflower seeds.

by not offering them more food until they have eaten the less tasty items remaining in their food dish or pantry.

Pellets

Some dwarf hamster owners also offer their pets nutritionally complete laboratory blocks or pellets made specifically for hamsters and other rodents. These types of food contain a balance of all the nutrients your dwarf hamsters need. They are convenient and easy to feed. The ingredients in these blocks are blended so that a hamster cannot pick out one ingredient, and he will therefore consume adequate nutrients. The blocks are usually low in fat, typically less than 5 percent compared to 40 percent fat in sunflower seeds. These lab blocks do not always fit in a dwarf hamster's cheek pouches and must be carried to their pantry. In addition to the lab blocks, your pets still need a hamster mix so they can engage in their natural behavior of carrying food in their cheek pouches to their pantry.

How Much to Feed

Your hamsters should always have food in their dish or in their pantry. Even though they are primarily nocturnal, your hamsters will still nibble on food during the day. The amount your hamsters eat will vary depending on what type of food you feed. Typically dwarf hamsters eat less of the laboratory blocks than they do of the rodent mixes. Every few days, check on your hamsters' pantry to ensure that the food is not damp or moldy, and be sure to discard stored food at each weekly cleaning.

When to Feed

It is best to feed your dwarf hamsters the same amount of food at the same time each day. Since hamsters are nocturnal and most active at night, you should feed your pets in the evening rather than in the morning. Try to feed your hamsters at the same time each day, such as when you come home from school or work, or after your own dinnertime.

Quick Tip

If your dwarf hamsters are housed in a wire cage, do not feed them through the cage bars. Otherwise, anything (including a finger) that is poked through the cage bars might get nipped. Always open the cage door to offer a treat. In addition, wash your hands before handling your hamsters, because any food smells on your hands can cause your hamsters to nip.

Food and Activity Levels

How much your hamsters need to eat will change throughout their lives. The amount will vary according to your pets' age, gender, and activity level. Young, growing hamsters will need to eat more food per gram of body weight than do adults. Because male dwarf hamsters are larger than females, they need to eat more food than females. Dwarf hamsters that run around and play with their toys will require more food than dwarf hamsters that just sit in their cage with no toys and little to do. Unless you weigh the amount of food

The amount of food your dwarf hamsters will need depends on their activity levels. Dwarf hamsters who are very active will need to eat more food than those who are not.

you feed your pets, you are unlikely to notice these differences because they are very small. However, pregnant or nursing hamsters obviously eat more food.

Treats

In addition to your hamsters' regular diet of grains, seeds, and laboratory blocks, you can offer your pets small amounts of fresh fruits and vegetables. Dwarf hamsters relish fruits and vegetables and can be given daily treats of small, well-washed pieces. Before offering these items, be sure to wash and dry them. Offer your

Hoarding

Ideally, your hamsters should immediately eat the fresh food items you offer them. However, many dwarf hamsters prefer to stuff the items into their cheek pouches and add them to their pantry. If your dwarf hamsters do not eat their fresh foods right away, they could spoil. Each evening, before you offer your pets more fresh food, check your pets' pantry and nest and remove any uneaten fresh items.

Quick & Easy Dwarf Hamster Care

Unhealthy Treats

While it can be fun to offer your dwarf hamsters new types of food and see if they enjoy them, not all foods are good for hamsters. Do not feed your dwarf hamsters junk food made for people. Although hamsters will greedily eat potato chips and eagerly look for more, potato chips, cookies, candy, and other snack foods are not healthy for your pets. Sweet, sticky foods, including moist, dried fruits, can become stuck in a hamster's cheek pouches and should not be offered. Also avoid feeding high-fat foods, such as the seed and nut mixes sold for parrots and cockatiels.

hamsters no more than one-half teaspoon each of fresh foods. By using this conservative estimate of the amount, your pets are less likely to experience any problems, such as diarrhea.

Dwarf hamsters enjoy eating hard vegetables and fruits such as carrots and apples. These foods are less likely to spoil than soft, moist items such as cucumbers and berries. Some dwarf hamsters also like green wheat shoots (sold as cat greens at pet stores). Hamsters that regularly consume fresh foods in their daily diet are less likely to experience digestive upset than hamsters that are rarely fed such foods.

Pet stores sell a variety of tasty treats for hamsters. Moderation is the key when feeding your hamsters treats. Your dwarf hamsters should not eat so many treats that they have no appetite for their regular food. Some treats sold at pet stores are designed to help create a more interesting environment for your hamsters. Seed treat sticks, hay cubes, and millet sprays (in the bird section of pet stores) hung in the cage keep hamsters busy. To prevent overindulgence, hang the treats in the cage for five or ten minutes and then remove them. Offer them again on the following evening.

Other treats to try offering your dwarf hamsters include dry, unsweetened cereals such as those made from oats, rice, and shredded wheat. Dwarf hamsters also enjoy eating pretzels, crackers, stale bread, uncooked noodles, uncooked rice, and uncooked hot cereals (for example, cracked four-grain cereal). Many dwarf hamsters love dog biscuits, but be cautious about offering any of your dog's regular kibble, as some brands are high in fat.

Live Foods

Dwarf hamsters enjoy eating live moths, mealworms, and crickets. Both crickets and mealworms are sold at pet stores for reptiles. It is fascinating to watch a hamster pounce on a mealworm or chase after and catch a cricket to eat. A dwarf hamster usually turns a mealworm or cricket in his hands so that he consumes the head first

Fresh fruits and vegetables are great treats for dwarf hamsters. Be sure to wash and dry them thoroughly, and you can offer small pieces to your pets daily.

Many dwarf hamsters enjoy live foods as treats, such as mealworms, crickets, or moths, which can be found in pet stores.

before eating the remainder of the insect. Not all dwarf hamsters will eat live foods; some hamsters become frightened and want nothing to do with insects. Feed live foods as a treat and offer only one or two every few days.

Water

Your dwarf hamsters should always have fresh water available. A dwarf hamster will typically drink less than 5 milliliters of water each day. The amount of water hamsters drink each day depends on the moisture in their food. If you provide your hamsters with small amounts of fresh fruits, vegetables, and live insect foods, they will drink less water.

Many water bottles are sold with milliliter or ounce markings on them. (There are approximately 29.5 milliliters in one ounce) Such markings are useful to track your hamsters' water consumption. If the amount of water in the bottle does not seem to decrease over a day or so, check to see whether the metal spout is clogged with bedding.

Feeding Your Dwarf Hamster

Ideally, you should change your hamsters' water every day, but at the very least, completely change the water in your hamsters' bottle once a week. It might be necessary to change the water more often if you have more than two hamsters in a cage. Select a water bottle that is large enough so that your hamsters do not run out of water. The standard hamster bottle provides sufficient water to last two hamsters for most of the week.

It is important to give the water bottle a good cleaning at least once a week. Even if the bottle looks clean, it is probably slimy on the inside and contaminated with bacteria and other harmful pathogens. Use a slender bristle brush to clean the slimy residue that will coat the bottle. Check to see that the stopper is not clogged with bedding. Some hamsters nibble the metal waterspout, so check to be sure there are no jagged ends that could cut your pets. If there are, you will need to replace the water bottle.

Taming & Grooming Your Dwarf Hamster

A tame dwarf hamster will let you hold and pick him up without becoming frightened. The time you spend holding and playing with your hamsters will help your pets learn to trust you and become tame. If your dwarf hamsters are sleeping when you want to play with them, call their names, tap on their nest box, and allow them a several minutes to wake up before you visit.

If you wake up your pet from a deep sleep, he will exhibit threatening behavior, such as rolling over on his back, baring his teeth, and perhaps growling and squawking. If you startle or grab your dwarf hamster before he is awake, he might bite you. Do not force your pets to come out of their nest box when they would clearly rather sleep. Begin your taming sessions in the early evening, when your hamsters are naturally awake. Establishing a routine, such as visiting with your hamsters at the same time each evening, can help with the taming process.

Some dwarf hamsters are very wiggly and active. If your pets exhibit such behavior, it is best to start taming them by keeping your hand inside their cage rather than taking your pets out of their cage. Let your hamsters sniff and crawl on your hand. Place a food treat in the palm of your hand and encourage them to climb onto your hand. Do not make rapid movements with your hands. If your hamsters seem confident, try petting your dwarf hamster along his side or behind his ear. Even a brief momentary stroke will work. Continue to slowly pet your hamsters within their cage while talking softly to them so they get used to your voice. Expect the taming process to take several weeks. Some timid or nippy individuals take more time and patience.

Always put your hand in your dwarf hamster's cage palm up; then pick him up by letting him climb onto your hand or by scooping him up under his belly.

Quick & Easy Dwarf Hamster Care

Start Out Slow

Dwarf hamsters do not like to be held for very long or to be restrained while being held. If you try to hold a dwarf hamster snugly in your hands, he will usually struggle and push through your fingers with his nose to try to get away. He might also try to bite you. Keep in mind that a normally docile hamster might bite you when he is frightened. Before taking your pet out of his cage, practice holding your hamster in his cage and make sure that he is used to you.

Holding Dwarf Hamsters

There are two methods that can be used to pick up your dwarf hamster. One is to use a container to scoop up your hamster, or, once he is tame, you can pick up your hamster by scooping him into both of your hands.

The cardboard roll from toilet paper is a good container with which to pick up your hamster. Hamsters do not like being scooped up in a glass container because the smooth sides do not let the hamster hold onto anything. Nonetheless, either container will work. Be sure the container you choose will easily fit into and out of the cage. Do not chase the hamsters around the cage with the container. Place the container on the cage floor near a corner and gently coax your hamster into the container. Cover the top of the container with one hand to prevent your hamster from leaping out.

Once your hamster is familiar with you and your hands, you can pick him up by letting him climb onto your hand or by scooping him up under his belly. Hamsters can be frightened when a hand descends down over their back, so always put your hand in their cage palm up, lower it to the bottom of the cage, then move it toward your hamster.

Fast Movers

Dwarf hamsters are nimble. Even after your hamster is calm and tame, always use two hands to hold him. Loud noises and sudden movements (your own or those caused by another person or pet) could scare your pet and cause him to jump out of your hands. Hamsters can also take unpredictable leaps from your hand.

Use one hand to hold your hamster and lightly cup you other hand over his back or in front of his face. Use one of your hands to block or control his movements. With especially active dwarf hamsters, you will probably have to continually walk your hamster between your hands. Keep your hamster close against your body for greater security. It is also prudent to immediately sit down when holding your hamster, so that if he does jump out of your lap, he will not fall as far as he would have if you were standing.

Many dwarf hamsters will stand up on their hind legs with their eyes alert and noses twitching when they are curious.

Dwarf Hamster Body Language

Understanding your hamster's body language can help you be more sensitive to your pet's moods and help you tame your pet better. You do not want to continue playing with your hamster if he becomes scared. When nervous, a hamster might wash his face. As part of the "flight or fight response," some frightened hamsters defecate or urinate. When frightened, your pet might flatten himself close to the ground, run away, or bite. If your pet does any of these behaviors, you should talk gently to him, then put him back into his house so that he can calm down.

During both play and fight, hamsters often push at each other with their front paws. You might also hear your pets squeak or softly grind their teeth together when they are angry and ready to fight. A submissive hamster will try to appease a more dominant animal by walking stiffly away with his tail up. Some happy hamsters spring and leap in the air. Curious hamsters will stand up on their hind legs, ears alert, and noses twitching, to investigate their surroundings.

Playtime

Dwarf hamsters are fun to just watch while they play in their cage. However, most pet owners want to take their hamsters out of their cage to play and explore. While other types of pets, such as rats, rabbits, and gerbils, can be allowed to safely explore and play in a "pet-proofed" room, dwarf hamsters are too small for such an activity. Dwarf hamsters are so small, they can squeeze into spaces that you are unlikely to notice until it is too late. In short, the chances of their escaping and becoming lost are great, and they are very difficult to recapture. Unlike the other types of small mammals or "pocket" pets, if dwarf hamsters disappear from sight they tend to hide rather than becoming playfully interactive with their pet owner.

Do not leave your pets unsupervised. Hamsters can quickly disappear until small nooks and crannies and be very hard to find.

Always supervise your pets closely if you take your dwarf hamsters out of the cage to play. Make sure the area is escape-proof and safe.

Hamsters also have no awareness of heights and will walk right off the edge of a bed, table, or chair, falling and potentially breaking a bone.

Other options for play outside your pets' cage include large plastic enclosures made especially for small pets that you can set up much like a child's playpen. A high-sided plastic swimming pool is suitable for a dwarf hamster playground. You can place the dwarf hamster's nest box and toys in the playground. Make sure that all of these enclosures are escape-proof.

A mouse-sized or dwarf hamster-sized plastic run-about-ball is another safe option for allowing hamsters to play outside of their cage. Only one dwarf hamster can be placed in a run-about-ball at a time. Some balls are designed to move on a racetrack, which helps to confine your dwarf hamster's movements to a safe place. Always supervise your dwarf hamsters when they are out of their cage, because stairs and other household pets are potential hazards.

Escapes

Despite all your precautions, your hamster might still escape from his cage or run away while you are holding him.

If your dwarf hamster escapes from his home, place the cage on the floor next to a wall and toss in a few treats. In time, your curious escapee will return home to investigate the treat and you can capture him. If you are housing more than one dwarf hamster in the cage, do not leave the cage door open, because the other hamster will join the wanderer. Instead, provide that hamster with a new nest box, take the old nest box along with the nesting material and place it on the floor outside and next to the cage. Sometimes the hamster will return to the cage area and then fall asleep inside his familiar nest box.

Dwarf hamsters can squeeze into very small nooks and crannies when left to play outside of their cage, so it is best to limit their playtime to inside the cage or a run-about-ball.

If you want to introduce a new dwarf hamster to your original pets, buy a younger dwarf hamster, because they are more readily accepted than adults.

Introducing Dwarf Hamsters to Each Other

If you ever get a new dwarf hamster that needs to be introduced to the original pet, you should follow the steps described below. Dwarf hamsters are territorial and usually do not accept an unfamiliar hamster. Adult hamsters placed together in a cage for the first time will fight.

Buy a younger hamster to increase the chances for success. Younger dwarf hamsters tend to be more readily accepted than another adult.

Several methods can be used to help the introduction go smoothly. Place your original dwarf hamster in a wire cage and put the new dwarf hamster in another wire cage. Slide the two cages together so the hamsters can smell each other through the cage bars. Alternatively, you can try dividing a wire cage or aquarium with a piece of heavy-gauge wire mesh. You must be certain to securely place the wire so that the weight of a hamster pressing against it will not cause the mesh to fall. If the mesh gives way, the hamsters could reach each other and they will fight. The spaces between the wire mesh should also be small enough that a hamster cannot push his nose through and bite the other hamster.

Over the next several days, switch the hamsters several times a day between the cages or sides of the cage. Usually the two hamsters will accept each other within several days. If they fight, you must continue switching them back and forth for several more days before once again housing them within the same cage. Carefully watch your dwarf hamsters for the first few days they share a home to make sure that they do not fight and have accepted each other. Any wounds from bites could indicate that the two hamsters still do not like each other. Providing two nesting boxes for your hamsters can reduce the likelihood of the hamsters fighting.

An important caution about introducing a new hamster to your current pet is the potential risk of also introducing an illness.

Dust Baths

Wild dwarf hamsters take dust baths to help keep themselves clean and to control external parasites. Some pet dwarf hamsters will also take dust baths. You can use chinchilla dust (usually volcanic ash) or bird gravel for this purpose. Use a container deep enough to hold about a half inch of dust and large enough so that the dwarf hamsters can somersault and flip around in the dust. A glass or hard plastic container with sides about two inches high works well. Place the dust bowl in the cage for a short time once a week. Replace the dust after two or three baths. It is very entertaining to watch hamsters take a dust bath.

Serious hobbyists who breed hamsters usually quarantine a new arrival from their other hamsters, even if the newcomer seems healthy. A quarantine period helps prevent the transmission of illness among hamsters. The new arrival is kept in a cage as far away as possible from the other animals. The quarantine period can last from two to four weeks. During this time, the new dwarf hamster's health is monitored. When the isolation period is over, the newcomer can be moved into the area containing the other hamsters, assuming it has exhibited no signs of ill health.

Grooming Your Dwarf Hamster

Dwarf hamsters do not need to be brushed or washed. Clean cages are one of the most important ways you can help your hamsters stay clean and well groomed. If your dwarf hamster is dirty and smells, it is usually because he has been living on dirty bedding. Instead of giving him a bath, clean the cage, provide fresh, sweet-smelling bedding, and allow the hamster to groom himself.

Dwarf hamsters are naturally clean. They spend up to 20 percent of their waking hours grooming themselves. A dwarf hamster uses his front paws to wash his face, delicately cleans each ear with his hind toes, nibbles clean his toes, and washes his front and backside. Hamsters will also groom each other, especially in places they cannot easily reach themselves. A hamster that cannot keep himself clean is probably sick and should be examined by a veterinarian.

Dwarf Hamster Health Care

A healthy dwarf hamster should have dense, shiny fur. His coat should be smooth and sleek, with no bald areas or flaky skin. The dwarf hamster's eyes should be clear and bright. Overall, your dwarf hamster should look solid and a little plump, and not thin or bony. He should be alert and seem active when he's awake.

Knowing a dwarf hamster's normal behavior will help you recognize when one of your pets might be sick. Experienced pet owners and breeders are adept at recognizing when a pet is ill. As you gain experience caring for your pets, especially if you develop a long-term interest, you will also become more proficient. Sick dwarf hamsters

generally present a similar range of symptoms. Obvious signs of illness include discharge from the eyes or nose. Sudden changes in behavior, such as lethargy, reduced appetite, and failure to groom, can also indicate illness. Signs of disease that are more difficult to detect include rough hair, hunched posture, and weight loss. You should pay particular attention if your dwarf hamster is sensitive when touched on a certain part of his body, as this could indicate an injury from being dropped or squeezed. Any of these symptoms suggest that something might be wrong with your dwarf hamster, and a visit to the veterinarian might be prudent.

Sudden changes in behavior can indicate illness, so pay attention to your dwarf hamster and know his normal behavior so you can recognize any changes.

Act Fast

Most hamsters that are sick need to be treated by a veterinarian immediately. This is especially important because pet owners often do not notice symptoms in their pet until the animal is very ill. By the time a pet owner realizes that their animal is unwell, the dwarf hamster has usually been sick for quite some time. In many such cases, treatment is difficult because the condition is so advanced at the time of detection. Although some diseases progress rapidly and an affected pet can die in 24 hours, early recognition of a sick hamster may mean the difference between life and death for your pet. Furthermore, keep in mind that the more sick a hamster is, the more likely he is to be traumatized from the procedures at a veterinarian's office.

Finding a Veterinarian

In order for your dwarf hamster to receive the proper treatment, he needs the correct diagnosis. A veterinarian who routinely treats rodents and has a special interest in their care is the best qualified and will most likely have the necessary, smaller-sized equipment. In order to locate a veterinarian who is knowledgeable about rodents, inquire at pet stores, critter clubs, rescue societies, and also at other veterinarians' offices. They may be able to give you a referral.

Discuss potential costs with your veterinarian beforehand, so you will have a better idea how much your hamster's care might cost. Although it might be difficult to put a price on your pet, in some cases, it might be necessary to decide how much you can afford to spend.

Stress and Your Dwarf Hamster
What is Stress?

Stress is a catch-all word for a variety of conditions that disturb or interfere with a dwarf hamster's normal physiological equilibrium. Because stress often leads to illness, it is frequently mentioned as a contributing factor to various diseases. Besides becoming sick, a hamster can exhibit signs of stress in other ways, such as

Signs of Illness in a Dwarf Hamster

If your dwarf hamster is showing any of these signs, he may be ill. Take him to the veterinarian as soon as possible.
- Not eating or drinking
- Lethargy
- Oversleeping
- Runny nose, weepy eyes
- Diarrhea
- Failure to groom himself
- Weight loss

nervousness, lack of appetite, hair loss, and loose droppings. It is useful for pet owners to be aware of what constitutes stress for their hamster.

A dwarf hamster can experience stress from pain and fear, when moving to a new cage, from a change in diet, and/or exposure to temperature fluctuations. The trip from a pet store or a breeder to a new home can be frightening and stressful for dwarf hamsters. Once they are in their new home, some hamsters settle down right away while others take longer to adjust.

Stressful situations can also include loud noises, changes in diet, overcrowding, and harassment by dogs, cats, ferrets, or other pets. Groups of hamsters housed together can fight and injure each other. Stress can be a major factor in the development of what might otherwise remain a dormant disease. Therefore, it is wise to minimize the stress in your dwarf hamster's life.

Causes of Illness

The ailments that might affect hamsters can be classified into four categories: trauma-induced injuries, infectious diseases, noninfectious diseases, and improper husbandry. The reasons that a

Watch for Wounds

Injuries from fighting among hamsters can sometimes occur. Because infection from bacteria is always possible when a hamster is bitten in a fight, clean any bloody injuries with warm water and an antiseptic or hydrogen peroxide. An abscess can develop at the site of a bite wound due to bacterial infection. Watch the wounds, and if you detect any prolonged swelling or sign of redness, take your hamster to the veterinarian.

Quick & Easy Dwarf Hamster Care

Broken bones are a potential hazard to dwarf hamsters, but proper handling and safe playing can help prevent these injuries from occurring.

hamster becomes sick are often a combination of factors from more than one category. For example, a poorly ventilated cage can create a noxious-smelling environment with high levels of ammonia that causes an outbreak of a latent respiratory disease. Numerous factors can affect how sick the dwarf hamster will get, including the hamster's age, dietary deficiencies, and whether the dwarf hamster is already sick with another illness.

Trauma-Induced Injuries

A traumatic injury is caused when a hamster is dropped, falls, or is squeezed while being held. If a dwarf hamster is injured, especially if he appears in pain, you should bring him to a veterinarian right away. The veterinarian can determine whether the injury can be treated or whether it is kinder to end the dwarf hamster's suffering. Sometimes, some trauma injuries (such as injured toes) get better despite no care. Broken bones are a potential hazard because hamsters can accidentally jump from your hands if something frightens them. Properly holding and playing with your hamsters can prevent such injuries from occurring.

Dwarf Hamster Health Care

Infectious Diseases

Infectious diseases can spread from one animal to another and are caused by bacteria, viruses, and protozoans. Sometimes, the diseases caused by these agents are subclinical, with signs of infection difficult to detect. Individual animals also differ in their resistance to infectious organisms. Some exposed animals never display any symptoms. However, stress or other bacterial or viral infections can cause a dwarf hamster to suddenly show symptoms. A single pet is less at risk for infectious diseases compared to a pet that is housed in close proximity to large numbers of other animals of the same species. Infectious diseases are often preventable through good husbandry.

Wet Tail

The technical name for wet tail is proliferative ieitis. Various bacteria have been implicated as the cause. The main symptom of wet tail is diarrhea, and young hamsters are the most susceptible. Severe dehydration can result, and your dwarf hamster may stop eating and drinking altogether. This disease is best treated by a veterinarian, who will prescribe antibiotics, administer fluids, and possibly force-feed the dwarf hamster. Over-the-counter medications can be effective for some types of diarrhea, but not diarrhea due to wet tail. Because you cannot know the cause of your pet's diarrhea, prompt veterinary treatment is important, because even with veterinary care this disease can be fatal.

Noninfectious Diseases and Ailments

Noninfectious diseases and other ailments are caused by common, everyday factors. Usually, they are not life-threatening ailments, but nonetheless, should be evaluated and treated by a veterinarian. Some common dwarf hamster ailments are discussed below.

Emergency Symptoms

If your dwarf hamster displays any of the following signs of illness, immediate veterinary attention is needed:

- Refusing to eat or drink
- Runny nose
- Labored or rapid breathing
- Paralysis
- Congestion
- Refusing to move around the cage or appears to be in pain when handled
- Changes in droppings

Impacted Cheek Pouches

Sometimes an item, such as fluffy bedding or unsuitable sticky food, becomes stuck to the dwarf hamster's cheek pouch's lining. A veterinarian can remove the items with forceps or by flushing the cheek pouch. If your dwarf hamster seems unable to empty his cheek pouches, as evidenced by lumpy pouches, veterinarian treatment is also necessary. Sharp items can pierce the hamster's cheek pouch, which can lead to infection, abscess, or an everted cheek pouch. Any of these conditions should be treated by a veterinarian.

Diabetes

Diabetes is a chronic disease caused by either insufficient production of insulin or by resistance of organs to the effects of insulin. This disease has been documented in Campbell's Russian hamsters. Symptoms include excessive thirst and copious urination. These species are affectively treated with regulation of diet and insulin injections. At this time, treatment options for dwarf hamsters are limited. Nonetheless, your veterinarian can best advise you on a course of treatment.

Problems can arise in even the most healthy dwarf hamster, so be sure to seek treatment from a veterinarian if you suspect illness or injury.

Glaucoma

Glaucoma affects a dwarf hamster's eyes and can result in blindness. A symptom of glaucoma is a cloudy film on the lens of the eye. This disease has been documented in Winter-white hamsters. There is no treatment for this affliction. Responsible breeders do not breed from affected hamsters. If you suspect that your dwarf hamster is having trouble seeing, take him to the veterinarian for a checkup.

Tooth Problems

Although not common, the teeth of some dwarf hamsters sometimes need veterinary attention due to malocclusion.

A healthy dwarf hamster should have dense, shiny fur, eyes that are clear and bright, and a plump solid body.

Dwarf Hamster Health Care

Malocclusion occurs when a dwarf hamster's incisor teeth do not meet properly, either because the teeth are overgrown or they are misaligned. A dwarf hamster's teeth can fail to meet and wear properly for several reasons. Malocclusion can be inherited, or it can be caused by trauma, infection, or improper diet (for example, if the hamster does not regularly eat foods hard enough to wear down his teeth). Even if you inspected the dwarf hamster's teeth before buying him, be aware that hereditary malocclusion is often not detectable in young hamsters. Even if the teeth appear normal at first, as the hamster grows, the teeth become misaligned.

Don't Play Vet

If your dwarf hamster is displaying signs of illness or just doesn't seem to be acting like his normal, perky self, take him to the veterinarian for a checkup. The vet will be able to diagnose and resolve any medical issues.

Hamsters with this condition eventually cannot eat, lose weight, and will die without treatment. Many show symptoms often referred to as "slobbers," which are threads of saliva around the mouth and sometimes wiped on the front paws. If you notice that your pet is not eating, you can check his incisors by pulling back his lips. An affected hamster should be taken to a veterinarian who will clip or file the hamster's teeth.

Resources

MAGAZINES

Critters USA
Fancy Publications, Inc.
3 Burroughs
Irvine, CA 92618
Phone: (888) 738-2665
Website: www.fancypubs.com

ORGANIZATIONS

American Rat, Mouse, and Hamster Society
Denise Boyce
8275 Westmore Road #30
San Diego, CA 92126
Phone: (619) 390-2903
Fax: (619) 390-5271
Website:
www.altpet.net/rodents/rats/ARMHS.html

American Pet Mouse and Hamster Owners and Breeders
John Jones
P.O. Box 610
Douglas City, CA 96024
Phone: (916) 778-0240
Email: johnpaul@snowcrest.net

California Hamster Association
23651 Dune Mear
Lake Forest, CA 92630
Email: calhamassoc@hotmail.com
Website:
www.geocities.com/CalHamAssoc

Hamster Fanciers of America
Samantha Pettingill
107 Savannah Drive West
Bear, DE 19701-1635
Website:
www.geocities.com/Heartland/Hills/
1327/main.html

National Hamster Council (UK)
P.O. Box 154
Rotherham, South Yorkshire S66 OFL
England
Email: hamstercouncil@bigfoot.com
Website: www.hamsters-uk.org

Rat, Mouse, and Hamster Fanciers
Silvia Butler
188 School Street
Danville, CA 94526
Email: Jstarkey@telis.org

WEB RESOURCES

Hamsterland
A website with everything you need to know about caring for your hamster.
Website: www.hamsterland.com

Electronic Zoo/ Net Vet—Rodents
Website:
Http://netvet.wustl.edu/rodents.htm

Pet Parade
Website: www.pet-parade.com

Pet Finder
Website: www.petfinder.org

RESCUE AND ADOPTION ORGANIZATIONS

The American Society for the Prevention of Cruelty to Animals
424 East 92nd Street
New York, NY 10128-6801
Phone: (212) 876-7700
Website: www.aspca.org
Email: information@aspca.org

The Humane Society of the United States (HSUS)
Companion Animals Section
2100 L Street, NJ
Washington DC 20037
(202) 452-1100
Website: www.hsus.org

EMERGENCY SERVICES

Animal Poison Hotline
Phone: (888) 232-8870

ASPCA Animal Poison Control Center
Phone: (888) 426-4435
Website: www.aspca.org

Index

Photo Credits

Bonnie Buys: 7, 31
M. Gilroy: 1, 3, 17, 30, 33, 36, 40, 43, 44, 48, 49, 54, 57, 60, 61
Marianne Mays: 18, 22, 24, 29
Susan Miller: 53
John Tyson: 21, 38, 46